THE RAW FOOD PROGRAM
WHY? WHEN? HOW?
LENGTH OF TIME OF
THE BLOOD CLEANSING REGIME

by
Debbie L. Hoffman, M.S.

Copyright © 1984
by
DEBBIE L. HOFFMAN, M.S.

All rights reserved. No part of this book may be reproduced, in any form, except by a reviewer, without permission in writing from the copyright owner.

Library of Congress Catalog Card Number: 84-061433

Soft Cover book: ISBN 0-941706-05-2

PROFESSIONAL PRESS PUBLISHING COMPANY
13115 Hunza Hill Terrace
Valley Center, Calif. 92082
(619) 749-1134/749-1135

DEDICATED
to my grandparents, Dr. J. M. and Trudie Hoffman,
who have been an inspiration to me
in encouraging me to study nutrition

ACKNOWLEDGMENTS

I wish to acknowledge the wonderful help of those who made this work possible: for the excellent secretarial work of Norleen Henderson; for help given me in research by my grandfather, Jay M. Hoffman, Ph.D.; for the editorial work of Alberta Davis; and for the encouragement and support of my husband, Mark.

Debbie L. Hoffman, M.S.

TABLE OF CONTENTS

	Page No.
A Word About the Author	1
Introduction	2
Foreword	4
Preface	6

CHAPTER

1	Why the Raw Food Program?	9
2	When is the Raw Food Regime Necessary?	13
3	How Does One Know What to Eat and Drink?	15
4	Wheat Grass Juice—A Great Blood Cleanser	19
5	Sprouting and Growing Seeds and Grain	23
6	For What Length of Time Should One Follow the Raw Food Program?	27
7	What Foods Should Not Be Eaten?	33
8	What You Should Know About Fasting	39
9	Seasonal Fruits, Nuts, and Vegetables	41
10	Recipes For the Raw Food Program	45

A WORD ABOUT THE AUTHOR

Debbie L. Hoffman has her bachelor and master's degrees in nutrition and is now working on her doctorate. She has completed a considerable amount of research work in the field of nutrition including a trip to Hunza land, where she also did research work.

Debbie was given the opportunity of being raised by her grandparents, Dr. Jay M. and Trudie Hoffman, who knew the critical position nutrition would play in her life. As a result of their dedicated efforts she enjoyed a childhood free of common childhood diseases. Imagine growing up free of chickenpox, acne, and so many other ailments suffered by many children.

While traveling through the United States and Canada conducting five day nutrition seminars with her grandparents, Debbie recognized her need to help people through her knowledge of nutrition. She realized she could help people to change their life style, find health and happiness, and regain control of their lives through proper nutrition—rather than passively accepting the fate of their genetics and environment.

Debbie has observed and researched the many nutritional programs and theories currently in use. Through her research and practice she has found that good nutrition plays a very important role in our lives. Wholistic medicine is a balance of the physical, as well as the mental and spiritual.

INTRODUCTION

By Bruce A. Sanderson, M.D.

Dr. Sanderson is Past President of the San Diego Biomedical Research Institute. He is currently Chief of the Department of Otolaryngology — Head and Neck Surgery at the Hillside Hospital in San Diego, California.

THE RAW FOOD PROGRAM

I have just finished reading this crisp, direct, and I know, effective method of correcting certain health problems. Debbie is following in the footsteps of her well known vegetarian-nutritionist grandfather, Dr. Jay M. Hoffman. Does this method really work? Yes, it does. When my daughter was working for the city schools in Riverside, California as a speech therapist, she caught an overwhelming viral infection from one of her young students. For months she was laid up in bed. We later found that she had a serious defect of her immune system and for this reason she will tend to catch infections much more easily than most people. At Dr. Hoffman's suggestion, we put her on the program as suggested in this book. It worked. It didn't happen all at once. It took months before she was able to be up and about and one year before she was able to be effectively employed again.

Now comes Debbie L. Hoffman, who is preparing herself to be a competent vegetarian nutritionist. It is only right and proper that we should give her every encouragement possible. Go! Go! Debbie!

FORWARD

By John Westerdahl, M.P.H., R.D.

John Westerdahl is a nutritionist and health educator at Castle Medical Center in Kailua, Hawaii. He is a registered dietitian specializing in preventive medicine and is a member of the American College of Sports Medicine.

Today modern nutrition research has documented the health benefits of following a vegetarian diet. Studies have shown that vegetarian populations have significantly fewer cases of heart disease, cancer and other chronic degenerative diseases as compared to populations whom consume the typical Western diet. This has been attributed to the high fiber, high complex carbohydrate and low fat diet enjoyed by most vegetarians.

Those of us health professionals who are in the field of preventive medicine are becoming more and more convinced of the preventive and therapeutic value of the vegetarian diet. This is particularly true when we see an ever increasing number of patients helped by following such a dietary program.

There are specific times and conditions in which a raw food type vegetarian diet may be highly recommended and advised. This special kind of vegetarian diet most closely represents the type of diet originally given to us by our Creator as illustrated in the Holy Scriptures (Genesis 1:29).

Initially embarking on a raw food vegetarian diet may at first seem difficult and confusing. *The Raw Food Program* by Debbie L. Hoffman can be used as a guide to help individuals follow such a specialized dietary regime. This book can help you get started. Those who feel that following a raw food diet is "boring" and "monotonous" will be surprised to discover how interesting and satisfying such a meal plan can be. Within the pages of the book, the reader will be delighted to find over a hundred delicious and nutritious vegetarian raw food recipes that can be simply prepared in the home.

The research and creative work that has gone into the preparation of *The Raw Food Program* will make this volume a valued addition to anyone's library. The benefits of a more healthful life can be achieved by following it's valuable health principles.

PREFACE

By Bruce W. Halstead, M.D.

Dr. Halstead is Director of the Halstead Preventive Medical Clinic in Colton, California. He is past President of the American Academy of Medical Preventics. In 1975 he was honored for his research in chelation therapy by the American Academy of Medical Preventics. He is the author of numerous scientific articles and books.

The field of nutrition as it relates to human health care is in the midst of many revolutionary advances, changes, and technical conflicts. It is an area of controversy with an enormous background of technical and all-too-frequently conflicting scientific data. There is now general recognition in the scientific community that nutrition plays a very vital role in the maintenance of human and animal health. The same can be said for plants.

Despite the obvious, American allopathic medicine has been dedicated to the furthering of surgery, radiation, and a plethora of highly toxic drug agents. Unfortunately, disease prevention in the United States has a very low order of priority. In fact, in terms of the medical school curricula it has been almost nonexistent. When viewed in the overall national health budget, which is now approaching $400 billion a year, which is in excess of ten percent of our gross national product, the expenditures in the field of actual health maintenance and disease prevention are ridiculously low. The health index of America has dropped to about twenty-third place.

This particular book deals with a topic that is timely and important to the American public. The question is frequently raised by the uninformed and uninitiated, "How do I get started in a good nutritional program? What dishes should I prepare and how do I go about preparing the kind of food that is really required by my family?" The purpose of this book, which has been well written by Debbie L. Hoffman, the granddaughter of a very noted nutritionist, Dr. Jay M. Hoffman, is to answer these and other questions. This book has made a valuable contribution to our knowledge in the field of nutrition and human health. I wish to congratulate Debbie for the time and effort that she has taken to assemble this material because I think that it will be of considerable value to those that follow its advice.

Bruce W. Halstead, M.D.
Colton, California

Chapter 1

WHY THE RAW FOOD PROGRAM?

In the United States over fifty-five percent die of blood-vascular and heart disease. Twenty-five percent die of cancer. Think of it! Eighty percent, or eight out of ten Americans, die from these two diseases alone. Will you be one of the eight?

In 1984, about 420,000 people will die of cancer in this country — that is about 1,150 people every day — that is about one person developing cancer nearly every minute. Cancer remains the plague of the 20th century. It now strikes one out of every four Americans.

If your bloodstream is clean, alkaline, free-flowing, and getting plenty of oxygen through to the tissues, your chances of getting disease will be significantly reduced.

The Good Book says, "The curse causeless shall not come." Prov. 26:2.

"Disease never comes without a cause. The way is prepared and disease invited by a disregard of the laws of health."[1] In other words, if you are sick and ailing, you have done something wrong in your way of living. You need to change your lifestyle.

One of the quickest ways to clean up your bloodstream and be healthy is the "Raw Food Program". The original diet of man was raw food. "And God said, 'See, I have given you every herb that yields seed which is on the face of all the earth, and every tree whose fruit yields seed; to you it shall be for food.'" Gen. 1:29. NKJV. Here we find that seeds or nuts and fruit were the original diet of man. There is no doubt that originally there was a greater variety of seeds, nuts and fruits. Some of our best seeds today are sunflower, pumpkin, chia, and sesame. We still have an abundance of many types of nuts. We also have many varieties of delicious fruits.

After sin entered the world, God told man, "Cursed is the ground for your sake; in toil you shall eat of it all the days of your life. Both thorns and thistles it shall bring forth for you, and you shall eat the herb of the field." Gen. 3:17, 18. NKJV. Thus, man was to work the soil and raise herbs, grains and vegetables, which were added to his diet. These additional foods were also eaten raw. Nowhere does it say they were to cook them. To illustrate, when wheat and other grain are fully ripe, not dry, you can roll the green pods between your hands, blow away the chaff, and eat the grain. It is soft, delicious, and nutritious. In those days, man lived many times longer than we do today.

I visited Hunza land where people live for over a hundred years and die of old age instead of disease. They eat mostly raw food because of a lack of wood. In the winter, when they have to burn wood to keep warm, they also cook over the fire. But even then, they eat a lot of dried fruit, of which apricots are their main staple food.

Raw food is live food containing all the vitamins, minerals and enzymes necessary for optimum health. Cooked or roasted food is dead food; many of the enzymes and water-soluble vitamins have been destroyed. Thus your cooked or roasted food is depleted of many of the life-sustaining nutrients needed for maintaining buoyant health and long life.

Some may say, "I could not enjoy raw food three times a day." However, if you turn to the recipes found in this book, you will be amazed at how good raw foods can be when prepared and eaten with delight. Try it; you will love it!

"In case of sickness, the cause should be ascertained, unhealthful conditions should be changed, wrong habits corrected. Then nature is to be assisted in her effort to expel impurities and to reestablish right conditions in the system."[2]

"The doctor of the future will give no medicine, but will interest his patients in the care of the human frame, in diet, and in the cause and prevention of disease." Thomas A. Edison.

Hippocrates, the father of medicine, wisely said some 2400 years ago, "Let food be your medicine."

"If the whole materia medica as now used could be sunk to the bottom of the sea, it would be better for mankind." Oliver Wendell Holmes.

"There are many ways of practicing the healing art; but there is only one way that Heaven approves...pure air, sunlight, abstemiousness, rest, exercise, proper diet, the use of water, trust in divine power, — these are the true remedies."[3]

---

[1] *Councils on Diets and Foods,* by Ellen G. White, p. 122.

[2] *Preventive Medicine,* by Ellen G. White, p. 68.

[3] Ibid., pp. 67-68.

The Best Six Doctors
The best six doctors anywhere
   And no one can deny it —
Are exercise and sleep and air
   Water, sunshine and diet.

These six will gladly attend,
   If only you are willing
Your ills they'll mend,
Your cares they'll tend
   And charge you not a shilling.

Author Unknown

Chapter 2

WHEN IS THE RAW FOOD REGIME NECESSARY?

When people are sick and ailing, the bloodstream must be cleansed. If your bloodstream is clean, alkaline, free-flowing, and getting plenty of oxygen through to the tissues, your chances of getting disease will be significantly reduced. If you are sick and ailing you must clean your bloodstream. The quickest way to do this is to go on a raw food regime.

Remember that disease never comes without a cause. To be healthy we must follow the natural laws of good health. This is illustrated on the next page for your edification.

Individuals suffering with blood-vascular and heart disease, cancer, arthritis, diabetes, hypoglycemia, chronic headaches, allergies, asthma, and a host of other diseases, may benefit by following a raw food regime. You have everything to gain and nothing to lose.

Chlorophyll, which is found in all green vegetables, is one of the best blood purifiers known. That is the reason wheat grass is so important. Along with wheat grass there is also celery and parsley, both of which are very high in chlorophyll.

According to the
JOURNAL OF HOME ECONOMICS, Vol. 17, No. 5:

Average Loss-By-Boiling

IRON 48%
CALCIUM 31.9%
PHOSPHORUS 46.4%
MAGNESIUM 44.7%

POTATO
Lost by Boiling 50%
CABBAGE
Lost by Boiling 40%
CARROT
Lost by Boiling 30%
APPLE Lost by peeling, boiling and coring   50%

Chapter 3

HOW DOES ONE KNOW
WHAT TO EAT AND DRINK?

There are many theories on food combinations, but most of them are without logic or foundation. In order for one to know what is right and what is wrong, he must have a full knowledge of "food chemistry in its relationship to body chemistry."

When one goes to the university to study medicine, "food chemistry in its relationship to body chemistry" is not taught. It is not in the medical curriculum. This is most unfortunate. My grandfather, who encouraged me to study nutrition, and who has been an inspiration to me, wrote a book entitled, "The Missing Link In the Medical Curriculum, Which is Food Chemistry In Its Relationship To Body Chemistry."

Herein is set forth all that you have to know about food combinations. First, let us understand how food is digested. All starches should be digested in the mouth. In the mouth the salivary glands secrete a diastatic enzyme called tyalin, a salivary amylase. When starches are digested in the mouth, they become sugar. This is one of the main reasons why you should chew your food thoroughly so that the starches can be digested in the mouth. Undigested starches interfere with digestion in the stomach. Remember the proverb, "Chew your food, your stomach has no teeth."

Proteins are digested in the stomach by the digestive juices which contain hydrochloric acid and pepsin. If any fats are eaten with protein, it retards digestion for hours because the digestive juices are water-soluble and cannot freely penetrate the fats.

Fats are digested in the small intestine by the bile which emulsifies the fat.

Some people say that you should not eat starch and protein at the same meal. This is not scientific because all starch food contains protein. All grains are considered starch, but they also contain protein. Even the lowly potato, which is mainly starch, also contains some protein. I am quite sure that if God made starches with protein, He knew it was good for food.

People forget, or do not know, that starch is digested in the mouth, and protein is digested in the stomach. If you chew some fresh wheat you will notice that the starch becomes a liquid sugar and all that is left in the mouth is the protein, which is the gluten. Some farmboys do this and chew the gluten like you would chewing gum. The starch is gone, but the protein is left. When you swallow the protein, the digestive juices in the stomach digest the protein. When food is properly chewed, there will not be any problem with starch and protein.

Never drink anything that has caffeine or theobromine in it. They are poisonous and should not be consumed. Coffee, tea, colas, and some sodas contain caffeine. Coffee also contains caffeol, which is the oil that gives the aroma and flavor to coffee, and which is considered a carcinogen, a cancer producing item. It usually affects the bladder more than anything else and, in some cases, causes cancer of the bladder.

Cocoa and chocolate contain theobromine which is detrimental to health. According to chemistry, caffeine and theobromine are twin sisters. Notice how closely they are related. The formula for caffeine is

$C_8H_{10}N_4O_2$, and theobromine is $C_7H_8N_4O_2$. Cocoa and chocolate also contain tannic acid and oxalic acid, which are detrimental to your health and should not be used.

The best beverages are pure, soft water, and fruit, or vegetable juice. If fruit juices are canned or bottled, they are too concentrated and should be diluted with half water. Vegetable juices do not have to be diluted with water. The greatest healers of all juices is wheat grass juice. This is explained in the following chapter.

APPROXIMATE NUTRITIONAL CONTENTS OF IMPORTANT JUICES

Juice	Protein %	Fat %	Carbohydrate %	Calories Per Pint	Calcium %	Magnesium %	Potassium %	Sodium %	Phosphorus %	Chlorine %	Sulphur %	Iron %	Silicon %	Manganese %	Copper %	IODINE % parts/billion
Beet (red)	1.6	0.1	9.7	220	0.140	0.130	1.770	0.485	0.210	0.290	0.090	0.004	0.009	0.008	0.001	230
Carrot	.1	0.4	9.3	217	0.225	0.100	1.540	0.385	0.205	0.195	0.110	0.003	0.007	0.0005	0.007	180
Celery	.1	0.1	3.3	89	0.390	0.140	1.460	0.645	0.230	0.665	0.140	0.003	0.008	0.0014	0.001	
Cucumber	1.1	0.2	3.1	84	0.050	0.045	0.700	0.050	0.105	0.150	0.155	0.002	0.013	0.0064	0.016	500
Romaine Lettuce	0.8	0.3	3.0	94	0.345	0.065	1.660	0.100	0.140	0.395	0.130	0.007	0.018	0.008	0.0001	650
Parsley	1.2	1.0	9.0	283	0.350	0.160	1.50	0.200	0.130	0.090	0.120	0.016		0.0012	0.015	
Tomato	3.5	0.4	4.0	112	0.055	0.065	1.335	0.060	0.145	0.145	0.070	0.002	0.009	0.0003	0.0005	350
Apple	0.9	0.1	12.5	250	0.035	0.040	0.640	0.055	0.060	0.025	0.030	0.002	0.006	0.0017	0.0008	
Coconut	.1	0.5	7.0	700	0.120	0.100	1.500	0.180	0.370	0.600	0.140			0.0001	0.0009	
Grape	1.4	12.5	19.2	462	0.055	0.045	0.530	0.025	0.050	0.010	0.045	0.0015	0.002	0.0001	0.0005	
Grapefruit	1.3	1.6	9.8	200	0.105	0.045	0.805	0.020	0.100	0.025	0.050	0.0014		0.0002	0.0001	
Lemon	.4	0.9	8.7	210	0.110	0.045	0.615	0.030	0.055	0.030	0.045	0.003		0.0003		
Orange	.6	0.1	13.0	265	0.120	0.055	0.905	0.060	0.090	0.025	0.050	0.002	0.0007	0.006	0.0008	
Pineapple	.4	0.3	9.7	207	0.040	0.050	1.350	0.080	0.055	0.255	0.045	0.002		0.0004		200

Chapter 4

WHEAT GRASS JUICE — A GREAT BLOOD CLEANSER

You cannot buy wheat grass or wheat grass juice and even if you could buy them, they are not the best. This is because they should be fresh. You should grow your own wheat grass which can be easily accomplished on a window sill, as follows:

1. Buy flat, non-metal cafeteria trays. Any size is suitable, but the best is 14 x 18 and approximately 1 inch deep.

2. Combine dark topsoil with potting soil, or peat moss. If you need to enrich this mixture, powdered kelp will enrich the soil. With a small flower sprinkler, moisten the soil.

3. Soak wheat kernels for 24 hours. During the day change the water and rinse the seeds every 4 hours. The wheat kernels should be soaked in a gallon jar and when rinsing, place a strainer (size of the jar opening) on top and let cold water from the faucet run forcefully through the strainer and into the jar for from one to two minutes. With the strainer on top of the jar, pour off the water.

4. Place the topsoil in the tray about 1 inch deep. Sprinkle the soaked seed evenly on top of the soil (avoid kernels bunching together). Cover with two or three paper towels. Moisten soil again as above, leaving paper towels in place, allowing the water to soak the towels. The soil should be moist and not saturated with water. Cover the top of the pan with a dark cloth or newspaper or serving tray or fiberboard. After 4 or 5 days, remove

the covers and place in front of a window. If necessary, add more water before putting the tray in front of the window. Alow the wheat to grow until it reaches 6 to 7 inches in height.

Cut the amount of grass needed to make the juice. To cut, use vegetable scissors or a serrated knife. Using a wheat grass juicer (Fig. 1), add the grass little by little. You may be able to purchase a wheat grass juicer in a health food store. If not, write to Sundance Industries, 28 Vermont Avenue, White Plains, New York 10606. Ask them for their brochure and price list. You may also phone them at Area Code 914-946-9340. I personally prefer the Wheatena Model S. It is not only the best juicer for wheat grass, but is also good for juicing other sprouts.

Wheat grass juice is very sweet and may make you feel a bit nauseous. It should therefore be diluted with pure, soft water. Distilled water is best for this purpose. In the beginning, put one tablespoon of wheat grass juice in a glass of water and drink it immediately. Drink a half hour before each meal and before going to bed. Increase the juice a little each until you reach two ounces of juice. Mix in a glass of water whenever you take the juice. Wheat grass juice for many years has been used as a detoxifier and blood cleaner. It is important for many degenerative diseases including cancer, by supplying important nutrients to the body.

Do not expect wonderful results overnight. Degenerative diseases are long-time in showing their insidious ailments. It takes time to get rid of them. Don't give up; persevere, and be patient. As the proverb goes, "Rome was not built in a day."

For those who cannot afford a machine for juicing

the wheat grass, the next best is wheat grass powder. Take a heaping teaspoon and place in a glassful of distilled water, letting it soak only five minutes. Mix and drink. Bear in mind that the raw wheat grass juice is the best for you.

Wheat grass, like alfalfa, is excellent due to its high content of chlorophyll, enzymes, vitamins and minerals. Few persons get adequate chlorophyll from their diet because they eat much cooked food. Chlorophyll is one of the greatest natural factors for cleansing the bloodstream and the entire body.

Let me make it quite clear that when purchasing wheat grass or alfalfa, be sure that the label reads *"low temperature dried"*. The conventional method of dehydrating wheat grass and alfalfa is so hot that it destroys the enzymes and much of the water-soluble vitamins. Enzymes are destroyed at 130 degrees Fahrenheit. When you buy wheat grass or alfalfa, you want to be sure that it is a live product which means that the enzymes and water-soluble vitamins are still in the product. If the health food store does not have it, tell them to order some for you from their distributor. Low temperature wheat grass and alfalfa are organically grown in the fertile Kaw River Valley of eastern Kansas. The brand name is Pines Distributors, International, Inc., P.O. Box 1107, 1040 E. 23rd St. Lawrence, Kansas 66044. The grass is dried at temperature below 106 degrees Fahrenheit by using a unique dehumidification process rather than heat. Thus the nutrient potencies of enzymes, water-soluble vitamins and flavor are better retained by the low temperature method, which is as close to fresh as technologically possible.

Wheat grass is delicious. You can sprinkle it freely on salads or chew it dry and drink it with a little water. It can be used to enhance flavor in breads, soups, stews and gravies, mixed in juices, or made into a delicious tea.

Chapter 5

SPROUTING AND GROWING SEEDS AND GRAIN

Science has discovered that sprouted seeds and grains are high in nutrients of vitamins, minerals and enzymes. Sprouts are raw food and can be used in salads, raw food entrees, raw food soups, raw food crackers, raw vegetable juices, raw food spreads for sandwiches, and many other raw food items.

Sprouts can also be made into juice and mixed with other vegetable juices. Fresh raw tomato juice, to which has been added a very small amount of juice from raw parsley, dill, onion, garlic, lemon, and a pinch of salt can be most delicious and nutritious. This is called a raw vegetable cocktail.

Raw juices are a live food. Cooked and canned juices are dead food lacking the life-giving nutrients. Some people do not like to prepare food; they would rather eat the dead food in a restaurant. What is the end result? It is sickness and, eventually, early death. One cannot expect buoyant health from dead food. Concerning my great grandfather, when anyone passed him the salad dish he would say, "That is for the cows." He died at an early age of 52 years, too young to die. Sprouted seeds and grains are most conducive to good health and long life. You should always have various kinds growing in your home. The best method for sprouting is to use a gallon jar (if you do not have one, you can buy them in a delicatessen store). Add a quart of water, then add a small quantity of seeds. The formula is as follows: Small-size seed (like alfalfa): one-quarter cup per one-quart of water. Medium-size seeds: one-half cup per one-quart of water. Large-size seeds: one cup per one quart of water.

Let the seeds soak for twenty-four hours. During this period change the water and rinse the seeds every four hours, except when you are sleeping. During the sleeping hours, if possible, place the jar in the refrigerator. The method of changing the water and rinsing the seeds is as follows:

1. When seed or grain is first soaked in the water, place a cheesecloth, or white porous sheet-cloth over the top of the jar opening, then place a rubber band around the cloth to keep the seeds in the jar.

2. In order to keep the seeds or grain fresh and free from spoilage, they must be cleaned every four hours as outlined above. To do this, place a strainer over the opening of the jar and pour out the water.

3. With a strainer on top of the jar, run the cold water full force through the strainer and into the jar. When the jar is filled with water, pour out water, repeating this step at least three times.

4. With the cloth on top of the opening, place the jar upside down at a 90 degree angle and allow the water to drain. This takes about 3 minutes.

5. Roll the jar side-wise around and around until all the seed sticks to the jar sides; let it lay on its side.

6. Between washings, cover the jar with a dark cloth for four days.

7. After four days, remove the dark cloth and place it in the window after rinsing seed and rolling the jar. Be sure to keep the jar on its side.

8. When all the sprout leaves are green, place them in the refrigerator while in the jar, or in an air-tight

plastic container or a zip plastic bag. These you can purchase in any supermarket.

There are other methods of sprouting, but I find this one to be the most economical and the best controlled method. See Chapter 9 for the raw food recipes.

Here is to your good health! Try it, you'll like it!

Chapter 6

FOR WHAT LENGTH OF TIME SHOULD ONE FOLLOW THE RAW FOOD PROGRAM?

There are few people who are willing to live on a raw food program for the rest of their lives. For the benefit of those who feel this way, let me state that it is not necessary to live on a raw food program the rest of your life. However, it is extremely important that you strictly follow this type of program if you have any severe ailments.

As stated before, in order to have good health, you must have a clean bloodstream. If your bloodstream is clean, alkaline, free-flowing, and getting plenty of oxygen through to the tissues, your chances of getting disease will be significantly reduced. If you are sick, you will become well and happy by cleansing the bloodstream.

However, with terminal cancer, you may or may not get well. But you have nothing to lose and all to gain by giving this method a try. Remember that raw wheat grass juice is the key when used in conjunction with the raw food program.

While on this program there must not be any cheating. You must follow it religiously. For good health and long life you should follow the Basic Program on page 38, at the end of this chapter.

After you are well you should continue on the program for from three to six more months. When you start to eat cooked food, you must adhere strictly to the changed program as follows:

1. Follow the Basic Program religiously.

2. Do not overcook your vegetables. They should be just as green when you remove them from the pot as they were before you cooked them.

3. When cooking vegetables, use a steam basket like the one illustrated here:

Put a little water in the pot. Let water boil and the steam will cook your vegetables. If the vegetables change their color during the cooking, then you have overcooked them.

4. Eat a large salad before you put any of the cooked foods on the table. This is important, because if you put cooked food on the table with the salad, the cooked food will be eaten while it is warm and then there will be no room in the stomach for a large salad. Keep the cooked foods off the table until everyone has eaten his or her salad.

5. A large vegetable salad can be made tasty, delicious and nutritious.

6. In a large bowl, put in small pieces of the suggested

items: sliced radishes, green onions (scallions), cucumbers, and peppers; finely cut parsley, grated carrots and celery; and lettuce cut in small pieces. Use any lettuce except iceberg head lettuce which is mostly white and lacking in chlorophyll and nutrients. Sprinkle some onion powder, garlic powder, powdered oregano, lemon juice, and Dr. Bronner's Bouillon on top of the salad. Toss together the above items. The lettuce is the last item you put in the bowl. Dr. Bronner's Bouillon can be purchased in the health food store.

For breakfast, eat a lot of raw fruit including melon. After the fruit, eat Seven-Grain Cereal sprinkled with three or four tablespons of wheat bran, sometimes called miller's bran. Then cut up and add sugar-free Soyagen soy milk, manufactured by Loma Linda Food Company, in powdered form. Mix with distilled water and follow the directions on the can. Put in a bottle and keep refrigerated. The Seven-Grain Cereal recipe listed here is for your convenience. Store and use as directed below.

SEVEN-GRAIN CEREAL
Mix together:

1 cut wheat kernels   1 cup barley
1 cup rye kernels   1 cup brown rice
1 cup oal kernels   1 cup millet
1 cup hulled buckwheat

(Note: When the recipe calls for "kernels" this means the whole grain. None of these grains should be purchased cut, crushed, or ground because as soon as this happens oxidation begins with subsequent vitamin loss.)

Soak 1 cup of the above mixture with one-half cup raw bran in 4 cups water overnight. (Do not soak in aluminum.) In the morning, add 1 tsp. salt (do not change the water). Bring to a boil, turn heat down low and let simmer for several hours, until the water is almost cooked out. Then add 1 cup raisins, one-half pint boiling water, mix thoroughly together, let stand until cool and place in lidded casserole in refrigerator. Serve as a breakfast cereal with milk. For a delicious taste, cut up a ripe banana on top of cereal.

Note: For best flavor, cook this cereal in a stoneware slow electric cooking crock. (The removable crock is preferable.) Place in crock, turn to low and let cook all day. Check to make sure it does not stick. Add water if needed. In later afternoon, add one-half pint of boiling water and 1 cup raisins, stir thoroughly, When cool place in a casserole dish in refrigerator.

The wheat grass juice must be continued as outlined before in this book. This is a must and should be continued so that the ailment does not reappear.

If at any time you notice or feel that the ailment is reappearing, then return immediately to the raw food program. By no means should you ever return to eating your old way that caused your ailment.

Remember the proverb, "An ounce of prevention is worth a pound of cure." In other words, do not let it happen, prevent it. Let the body, mind and spirit prevail. Wholistic medicine means the whole body, mind and spirit as illustrated below.

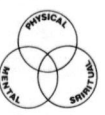

Wholistic medicine is actually preventive medicine. God wants all of us to adhere to the laws of health. He says, "Beloved, I wish above all things that thou mayest prosper and be in health, even as they soul prospereth." 3 John: 2.

BASIC PROGRAM

Follow these instructions religiously. They are the body's natural basis for achieving and maintaining optimum health!

NO!!	NO!!	NO!!
Sugar	Theobromine	Caffeine
White Flour	Cocoa	Coffee
White Rice	Chocolate	Tea
Sugared Cereals		Cola
Alcohol		Soft Drinks

Eat nothing made with any of the items above. Please read your labels before you buy.

NOTICE!! IMPORTANT!!

1. Exercise one-half hour every day.

2. Sleep 9 hours every night

3. Do not eat any dead flesh.

4. If constipated, make acidophilus yogurt, take it with every meal, and increase fiber in your diet (2-3 tablespoons bran daily).

5. Drink 2 glasses of water or juice one-half hour before meals.

6. Drink 1 glass of water or juice three hours after meals.

7. No oil, fat or grease.

8. No oxalic acid food.

9. No junk food.

10. Eat food containing fiber.

11. Lie in sun 30 minutes daily (15 mins. front, 15 mins. back — do not sunburn; fair-skinned people, total 10 mins., gradually increase.)

12. Take time to pray.

Chapter 7

WHAT FOODS SHOULD NOT BE EATEN?

All acid forming foods should not be eaten. Check my grandfather's Food Chemistry Chart which lists all the foods and what you need to know about them. Instructions are also on the chart so that you will know how to use it. Write to the publisher of this book for a list of all their works and price lists of same.

You should learn the difference between acid-forming foods and alkaline or base-forming foods.

Acid-forming foods thicken the blood and put a strain on the arteries and heart. Therefore, it is best to eliminate all of the high acid-forming foods, with the exception of eggs. Eggs are also high in albumen and cholesterol. They should never be eaten fried, poached, biled, baked, as omelettes, and so forth. They should only be used in the baking of roasts and cakes wherever needed as a binder. Whenever possible, buy eggs from a farm that does not coop the chickens up or feed them antibiotics.

You have heard it said that if an individual has an acid condition, all citrus fruits and tomatoes should be eliminated from his diet. This assumption has come from the fact that citric acid is an acid and therefore it will increase the acidity of the body. But his is not true. Citric acid is metabolized in the body and becomes an alkaline ash, or base-forming food. Notice the alkaline ash content of tomatoes and citrus fruits:

Limes	24.6 %
Tomatoes	24.5 percent
Oranges	23.4 percent
Lemons	21.4 percent
Grapefruit	12.3 percent

Since citric acid is metabolized in the body and becomes an alkaline ash, taking citrus fruit away from someone who has an acid condition would be taking away the very thing which would help to get rid of the acid condition. Again, people with an acid condition should eliminate from their diet all acid-forming foods in order to hasten the recovery from an acid condition.

OXALIC ACID: Oxalic acid foods should be avoided as the body cannot metabolize them. In order for the body to get rid of oxalic acid it calls for a reserve of calcium. If there is no reserve in the body, it will take it from the bones because oxalic acid must unite with calcium to form tiny, minute crystals called calcium oxalate. Normal kidneys will extract these crystals from the bloodstream, provided they are not overloaded with too many of them. If the kidneys are weak or overloaded with to many calcium oxalate crystals, then kidney stones may form. If an individual is eating too much food containing cholesterol, such as eggs, then he may develop gallstones. This is because the main components of gallstones are calcium oxalate and cholesterol, whereas kidney stones are mainly calcium oxalate. Therefore, oxalic acid foods should be avoided.

So far as spinach is concerned, this is only good for Popeye and not for human beings. Some say you can get rid of the oxalic acid by parboiling the spinach, while others say eat it raw. Both of these theories are wrong. Whether it is cooked or raw, it still contains oxalic acid and should not be used. Most of these items ought to be classified as weeds, and not as vegetables.

Take note of the following chart showing the amount of oxalic acid found in some foods.

OXALIC ACID
In % Milligrams per 100 grams (3 1/3 ounces)

Lamb's Quarters	11.10	Pokeweed	4.76
Beet Greens	9.16	Cocoa	4.50
Parslane Leaves	9.10	Sorrel	3.63
Spinach	8.92	Black Pepper	3.25
Swiss Chard	6.45	Tea—steeped 5 mins.	2.06
Rhubard Stems	5.00		

PEANUT BUTTER: Dr. John Harvey Kellogg invented peanut butter. Before he found out how harmful it was, it had spread over the country and he could not stem the tide. He found that roasted peanut butter interferes with digestion. He had been feeding it to the patients at the Battle Creek Sanitarium and Hospital. When he found out how detrimental it was, he decided to make peanut butter from steamed peanuts, or those that had been cooked like beans. After they were soft and tender he would grind them up the same way as the roasted peanuts. The difference was that in the roasted peanuts, the oil floated on the top. With the steamed peanuts, no oil came to the top because it was water-soluble.

MONOSODIUM GLUTAMATE (MSG): I would not use monosodium glutamate in my home because of the syndrome that occurred to me after eating in a Polynesian restaurant, as in the following description:

"Monosodium glutamate (MSG) has long been used to enhance the flavor of foods and is commonly included in commercially processed foods in the United States in amounts of 0.1-0.6 percent by weight. In 1968 a syndrome associated with eating Chinese food was reported. It was described as a feeling of numbness over the back of the neck and back, weakness, and palpitation, lasting up to two hours but leaving no after effects. It appears that the syndrome occurs when the concentration of MSG in the blood exceeds a threshold level, which differs among individuals. Concern about possible adverse effects from glutamate ingestion has been expressed because of the observations that subcutaneous injection of 4-8g/kg of sodium L-glutamate into neonatal mice produced changes in the retina.... Although large doses of MSG administered to neonatal animals with a slowly developing nervous system will produce retinal and neuropathological lesions, other species with more developed nervous systems are more resistant. The observations on both children and adult man indicate that human tolerance for this amino acid is high."[1]

SODIUM CHLORIDE — SALT: Sodium appears in its organic form in practically all fruits and vegetables. The amount of sodium in them will not cause trouble, because that amount of sodium in organic form is needed by the body. Some physicians tell people not to eat celery because it is too high in sodium. For your edification, organic sodium is not harmful. Inorganic sodium chloride is the culprit that causes the damage. "That sodium chloride might have harmful effects if eaten in excess was suspected long before any objective evidence on the subject existed. The association with hypertension proved more subtle. The effect of salt restriction in human hypertension, however, is now very well documented."[2] People with heart ailments and high blood pressure should eliminate sodium chloride from their diet. One of the biggest problems with people today is that before they even taste food, they start putting salt on it. This is a very bad habit. In fact, it would be better if the salt shaker were never put to the table. Enough salt is put in the food while cooking.

FLAX SEED: Flax seed is not a grain. It comes from the flax weed, from which comes linseed oil. Some bakeries put ground flax seed in the bread; others put it in cereals. Those who do this do not know food chemistry. They do not know that flax seed contains cyanide. "Poisonous Principle. The leaves and seed chaff contain the cyanogenetic clycoside, linamarin. An enzyme (linamarase) is present in the plant material which is capable of releasing cyanide from inamarin. . . Toxicity, Symptoms, and Lesions. In the world literature, cases of poisoning after ingestion of linseed press cake, press meal, or flaxseed chaff or screenings have been reported in all classes of livestock. Symptoms and lesions are those of cyanide poisoning."[3] We would all do well to warn the bakeries, cereal manufacturers and others who sell flax seed as a food that this item contains cyanide and should not be put in food. It can be used as a poultice on the outside of the body, but should never be taken internally.

[1] National Academy of Sciences, Toxicants Occurring Naturally in Foods, pp. 140-1.
[2] Ibid., p. 29
[3] John M. Kingsbury, Poisonous Plants of the United States and Canada, pp. 198-9.

Chapter 8

WHAT YOU SHOULD KNOW ABOUT FASTING

Proper fasting can be a blessing, but improper fasting can be a calamity. When you acquire a knowledge of food chemistry in its relationship to body chemistry, then you understand what happens internally. It is most important that we all should understand this. When you eat or drink something what happens inside of your body? How are the digestive organs affected? How is the bloodstream, the arteries, and the heart affected? How are the various glands affected? How are the nerves and brain affected? Many more questions could be asked on this subject.

Now let us find out what happens when you fast. After two days, if a person fasts only on water, he or she is living on his or her own broken down tissues and other waste materials. These waste products are acid and thicken the blood, placing a strain on the kidneys, arteries and the heart. It is for this reason that some people have heart attacks while on a water fast. Dr. Richard Passwater states in this book: *The No-Flab Diet*, that this acid condition called ketosis has other side effects such as fatigue, weakness, dizziness, irritability, insomnia, and in rare cases, coma.

How can we expect a dirty bloodstream to cleanse the tissues when the blood is thick and on the acid side. Can you imagine a woman washing her clothes in muddy water and expecting them to come out clean? Or, could you expect a woman to wash her dishes in muddy water and expect them to come out clean? The answer is quite obvious. No! The clothes will not be clean; the dishes will not be clean. And, anyone who is on a fast of water only is not going to be able to clean the bloodstream and the tissues and get plenty of oxygen through to the tissues.

If a person wants to fast after two days on water, he should fast on celery and carrot juice. Half and half of each. These items are alkaline and keep the blood clean and free-flowing. Now the bloodstream can carry plenty of oxygen to the tissues which need 45 percent at all times. The alkaline, or base-forming foods of celery and carrots, are as follows:

Celery .... 93.8 percent alkaline ash
Carrots .... 33.5 percent alkaline ash

This means that the blood is kept clean, alkaline, free-flowing, and getting plenty of oxygen through to the tissues. If need be, you can add a little wheat grass juice or 1 heaping teaspoon of low-temperature dried wheat grass to each glass of carrot and celery juice. For those who want to fast, this is the only safe method.

Chapter 9

SEASONAL FRUITS, NUTS, AND VEGETABLES

Spring

Apples, Bananas, Oranges, Strawberries, Cherries, Apricots

Walnuts, Almonds, Hazelnuts, Sunflower Seeds

Red Radishes, Beets, Cauliflower, Tomatoes, Corn, Lettuce, Peas, Cabbage, Parsley, Carrots, Dandelion, Kohlrabi, Watercress, Avocado

Summer

Apples, Peaches, Apricots, Cherries, Strawberries, Raspberries, Plums, Pears, Watermelons, Cantelopes

Almonds, Hazelnuts, Pecans, Sunflower Seeds

Lettuce, Celery, Tomatoes, Cauliflower, Carrots, Onions, Peas, Cabbage, Cucumber, Corn, Beans, Parsley, Kohlrabi, Avocado

Autumn

Pears, Grapes, Peaches, Plums, Apples, Bananas

Almonds, Hazelnuts

Eggplant, Leeks, Carrots, Parsley, Lettuce, Beets, Cabbage, Tomatoes, Onions, Cucumber, Corn

Winter

Tangerines, Pears, Apples, Oranges, Grapes, Bananas

Almonds, Hazelnuts, Walnuts

Brussel sprouts, Tomatoes, Endive, Carrots, Artichokes, Leeks, Lettuce, Turnips, Celery, Cucumber, Cauliflower, Avocado

MASTICATION

The stomach has no teeth. Teeth were the product of necessity. They were placed in the mouth by nature for the specific purpose of emulsifying food, so that it could be absorbed by the body. This process we call digestion.

Food that is not thoroughly pulverized by mastication must be reduced to solution by the stomach and the other digestive organs. If it be such material as the gastric juice will not dissolve, then it must be disposed of by disintegration, which starts with fermentation.

This is the genesis of nearly all ingestion and intestinal disorders.

Fermentation changes food from a life-giving to a life-destroying substance. It generates a poisonous gas which is absorbed by the system and which preys upon the red corpuscles of the blood, lowering the vitality of every organ of the body.

This is only one of the many evils that result from imperfect mastication. A whole book could be written and the subject not exhausted — in fact, a very admirable work has been written by Horace Fletcher called "The ABC of Our Own Nutrition," devoted almost entirely to the subject of mastication.

Nature is a perfect economist. If the teeth are not used, she will refuse to keep them in repair; she will allow them to decay. She presumes that you do not need them because you have refused to put them to that use for which they were created. So long as people subsist upon soft, cooked, mushy foods, they cannot expect to have good teeth. This is one of the greatest arguments against the baneful habit of cooking and in favor of elementary foods.

Nature produces no food that should be swallowed without mastication, when eaten in its elementary state.

Perfect mastication is the surest means of avoiding the habit of over-eating, which is so disastrous to the health and so common among civilized people.

Chapter 10

RECIPES FOR THE RAW FOOD PROGRAM

Before you start: Remember we have a responsibility to eat properly. We owe it to ourselves to seek and attain the highest degree of health possible. We start this by following certain basic rules for eating. These rules have been verified by modern research and are followed in all cultures where long life is the rule rather than the exception.

When considering food selection, at all times choose nutritive foods rather than "empty calories". Pass by the refined foods and opt for whole grain and natural foods.

Prepare your food with care. It should be cleaned well. If not removed from your food, dirt and grit can be harmful. Genuine home food preparation is a means of obtaining good health.

Proper eating is just as important as preparing the food with care. Each mouthful should be chewed slowly and completely. Care should be taken to remove external distractions such as the television, telephone and newspaper. It is best if you can relax a few minutes before eating to allow release of any tension so that your meal can be properly digested.

You will tend to eat less when essential nutrients are being supplied through good quality food rather than "junk food". Proper food preparation and eating are the cornerstones of physical well-being.

The Raw Food Program does not eliminate baked items, providing the heat never goes over 110 degrees Fahrenheit. Enzymes and some water-soluble vitamins are destroyed at 130 degrees Fahrenheit. For homes that have an electric warmer, it is easy to control the heat and keep it between 105 and 110 degrees.

At this low degree of heat, you will have to double the baking time. The items baked will not be as thoroughly baked as they would be at high temperatures. The important thing to remember is that most of the enzymes and water-soluble vitamins are still active — otherwise, you are not on a raw food program.

Be sure to use an oven or refrigerator thermometer and watch closely so the heat does not go over 110 degrees. It is best to test your oven or warmer when it is empty and mark the setting that keeps the heat between 105 and 110 degrees. Some people bake their raw food on a stone that is heated by the sun. This is fine if the heat does not go over the degrees as stated above.

RECIPES

In bringing about any change in the habits of people, it becomes necessary to pursue lines of least resistance. So firmly fixed in the minds of the public is the idea that foods need preparation, need fixing or something done to them before they can be eaten, that in order to induce them to take any step in the direction of correct feeding it becomes necessary to in some way prepare even elementary, or foods in their natural condition. In reality foods in their natural condition require but little preparation.

The recipes given here prove that there is a far wider scope for variety and display than most people would suppose. They are the results of long, careful and tedious experimenting. They are offered as a help to those who desire to take up the new or natural method of living.

The recipes given here we regard as little more than suggestions. We sincerely hope that those who deem it worth their while to give any thought to the kind of material out of which they build their bodies and brain, will take up this great work and carry it on to higher and higher degrees of development.

Difference in temperature is the only scale by which to measure motion, or all expressions of energy. Food, therefore, should never be eaten very cold nor very hot, but as near the temperature of the body as possible, cold food must be brought to the temperature of the body at the expense of energy. Icy drinks are responsible for such stomach trouble. They do violence to every law governing health.

APPETIZERS

AVOCADO STICKS

1 Avocado, mashed
Celery stalks
1 tablespoon Bronner's Bouillon
2 tablespoon Tofu mayonnaise
1 teaspoon garlic powder
Tomato and zucchini: optional

Combine avocado, bouillon, mayonnaise and garlic powder. Stuff mixture into celery stalks. Serve with zucchini sticks and tomato wedges on bed of lettuce if desired.

AVOCADO TREAT

½ Avocado per person
½ Diced Apple per person
1 Chopped Pineapple Ring per person
3 Chopped Half Walnuts per person
Shredded Coconut

Mix apples, pineaple and walnuts. Turn into avocado half. Sprinkle shredded coconut on top and serve.

BRAN STUFFED TOMATOS

2 Tomatos
6 Sprigs chopped parsley
1 Small onion, diced
¼ cup cucumber, diced
Lettuce
¼ cup cabbage
1 tablespoon Millers Bran per person
1 tablespoon Lemon juice per person
1 tablespoon Bronner's Bouillon

Mix all ingredients thoroughly and stuff into tomato. Refrigerate 1-2 hours and serve.

GUACAMOLE

3 avocados, mashed
Juice of ½ lemon
2 green onions, finely chopped
½ cup tofu mayonnaise

Combine all ingredients. Put on a bed of shredded lettuce and place wedges of carrot, celery and zucchini sticks around it.

MOCK SUSHI

1 Head Romaine lettuce
2 Cups alfalfa sprouts
1 Cup lentil sprouts
½ Cup wheat sprouts
1-2 avocados, mashed
1 Garlic clove, minced
3 tablespoon Bronner's Bouillon
1 Lemon, juiced

Thoroughly blend or mash all ingredients except Romaine. Strip the center core from each lettuce leaf. Over-lap the two halves and spread a layer of filling on top. Roll up and secure with a toothpick. Refrigerate 1-2 hours. Serve whole or sliced.

SESAME STICKS

Celery
Almond or raw peanut butter
White Sesame Seeds
Carrot sticks, optional

Stuff celery stalks with nut butter and then sprinkle the seeds over each stalk. For color and added nutrition, add carrot sticks and serve on bed of lettuce.

STUFFED CELERY

6 celery stalks
raw peanut butter
raw sesame seeds

Spread the peanut butter into the groove of each stalk with a butter knife. Run the flat part of the knive over the top of each stalk for evenness. Sprinkle with sesame seeds and serve.

STUFFED MUSHROOMS

1 dozen mushrooms
1 cup chopped pecans
¼ cup pecan meal
3 green onions, finely chopped

Rinse and scrub mushrooms, remove stems and chop. Set aside caps. Add chopped stems to the chopped pecans, green onion and mayonnaise. Stuff mixture into mushroom caps and garnish each top with a small amount of pecan meal.

VEGETABLE MARINATE

2 Cups chopped Zucchini
2 chopped Tomatoes
2 Chopped Scallions
1 Minced Garlic Clove
1 teaspoon garlic powder
1 teaspoon oregano
1 Cup lemon juice
1 tablespoon Bronner's Bouillon

Combine all ingredients and mix thoroughly. Refrigerate 1-2 hours before serving.

VEGETABLE PATE

1 cup ground Almonds
1 cup ground Walnuts
1 cup ground Pumpkin Seeds
1 cup Raw Sesame Seeds
½ cup chopped Bell Pepper
1 cup fresh cut corn
1 cup Tofu Mayonnaise
6 Chopped Tomatoes
4 Chopped Scallions
4 tablespoon Bronner's Bouillon
1 Lemon, juiced

Mix all ingredients together and press firmly into a jello mould. Chill until firm and serve on bed of lettuce.

BREAKFAST SUGGESTIONS

Liquify:

2 pears
1 orange, peeled
½ banana
¼ cup raw pecans
1 tablespoon honey

Add and soak in refrigerator overnight:

1 cup chopped walnuts
1 cup rolled oats

Serve in bowls.

PROTEIN BREAKFAST CEREAL

1 cup sesame seeds (hulled)
1 cup pumpkin seeds
1 cup sunflower seeds
1 cup chia seeds

Mix the above in a jar with a wide opening. Grind fresh each morning ⅓ to ½ cup per serving in a Moulinex grinder. (NOTE: After using Moulinex, be sure to pull plug out of the socket before cleaning.) Do not grind all the seeds at one time, you can grind a little at a time until you have the complete serving ground up. Add milk, and fruit if desired, or milk and the IRON RECIPE.

ENTREES

CASHEW ALMOND BLANKETS

1 cup cashews, ground
1 cup almonds, ground
1 cup shredded carrots
1 cup raisins
finely chopped parsley
steamed cabbage
lemon

Combine all ingredients except the cabbage and lemon. Form into patties. Use the cabbage leaves to fold around the patties. Place on serving platter and garnish with lemon wedges.

CAULIFLOWER LOAF

3 cups cauliflower, finely chopped
1 cup raw almond butter
1 cup shredded carrots
Sprouts

Line bottom of non-aluminum pan with 1 cup chopped parsley. Combine all ingredients and put into loaf pan. Top loaf with 1 cup raw sesame or sunflower seeds. Chill for one hour in refrigerator. Invert loaf onto dish. Slice and serve.

CAULIFLOWER MUSHROOM PATTIES

2 cups cauliflower, chopped
1 cup mushrooms, diced
½ cup celery, finely chopped
3 green onions, finely chopped
½ cup raw peanut butter
1½ tablespoon Bronner's Bouillon
Lettuce, parsley

Put cauliflower through food grinder. Add cauliflower to mushrooms, onion and celery. Add remaining ingredients except lettuce and parsley. Form into patties. Serve on bed of lettuce and garnish with parsley.

LENTIL BURGERS

1 cup soaked lentils
1 cup fresh corn
1 green onion, chopped
½ cup raw peanut butter
1 cup chopped celery
1 tablespoon Bronner's Bouillon
1 tablespoon garlic powder

Soak lentils in warm water for four hours or overnight. Put lentils, corn, onion and celery through food grinder. Add other ingredients and mix together. Form into patties and serve.

MOCK SALMON LOAF

2 cups carrots, ground
2 stalks celery, ground
3 tablespoons raw peanut butter
¼ cup sunflower seed meal

Combine all ingredients and form into patties. Add onion powder and garlic powder to season. Serve with grated turnips or beets.

MUSHROOM BALLS

3 cups mushrooms, minced
1 cup almond butter
1 tablespoon minced garlic
1 tablespoon Bronner's Bouillon
Sesame seeds

Combine all ingredients except sesame seeds and form into balls. Roll each ball on sesame seeds. Serve on a bed of lettuce with either sliced tomato halves or sliced red radishes.

MUSHROOM LOAF

3 Chopped mushrooms
1 cup chopped celery
1 cup raw peanut meal
2 Mashed Avocados
2 medium tomatoes
2 Scallions, chopped
2 chopped garlic cloves
½ teaspoon oregano

Blend avocados, tomatoes, scallions, garlic, oregano. Pour mixture over mushrooms, celery and peanut meal. Put into glass loaf dish and refrigerate 1-2 hours or until ready to serve. Turn out of pan and serve.

NUT PATTIES

1 cup cashew butter
1 cup ground almonds
1 cup ground walnuts
1 cup ground pecans
1 cup ground peanuts
Minced parsley
Walnuts

Combine all nuts and cashew butter to make patties. Cover each patty with parsley and place a walnut half on top center of each. Serve on bed of lettuce. Can be served with slices of avocado, squash, tomato and cucumber.

NUTTY CROQUETTES

1½ cup Sunflower seed meal
1½ cup Almond meal
1½ cup raw peanut meal
½ Doz. diced mushrooms
3 Green onions, minced
½ cup parsley
3 Celery stalks, diced
1 Clove garlic, diced
3 tablespoon Bronner's Bouillon
1 tablespoon Caraway Seed
Lettuce
1 Doz. radish flowerettes

Mix all ingredients except lettuce and radishes and form into croquettes. Place on serving platter on bed of lettuce. To make radish flowerettes, use a knife to cut 4 petals into each radish. Soak in water 1-2 hours until the petals open.

OATMEAL PATTIES

2 cups ground pecans
1 cup oatmeal flour
2 cloves garlic, minced
1 small onion
1 tablespoon Bronner's Bouillon
2 zucchini squash

Combine all ingredients except zucchini. Form into patties. Place on serving platter with zucchini wedges as garnish.

SPROUTED CHICKEN PATTIES

3 cups lentil sprouts
1 cup raw almond butter
1 cup raw peanut butter
2 cups celery, minced
2 cups fresh cut corn
1 cup yellow pea sprouts
3 green onions, minced
2 tablespoon Bronner's Bouillon
Parsley
2 carrots, sliced

Put sprouts, corn, celery and onions in food grinder. Add almond butter, peanut butter and bouillon. Mix well. Form into patties and garnish with parsley sprigs and carrot slices.

SPROUTED GARBANZO CROQUETTES

1 cup sprouted garbanzo beans, mashed
¼ cup parsley, finely chopped
½ cup Carrots, juice with pulp
½ cup green onion, minced
½ cup celery, minced
1 teaspoon onion powder
1 tablespoon Bronner's Bouillon
½ cup raw sesame seeds

Combine all ingredients except the seeds and form into balls. Roll in seeds and serve on bed of lettuce.

STUFFED PEPPERS

1 cup sprouted wheat berries
1 cup sprouted rye or sunflower seeds
½ cup shredded carrots
½ cup Chopped celery
½ cup ground cashews
2 tablespoon Bronner's bouillon
1 Small onion, chopped
4 Whole peppers, cleaned with tops cut off

Combine all ingredients and stuff into peppers. Put in refrigerator and chill before serving.

STUFFED ZUCCHINI

2 medium Zucchini

STUFFING
2 cups sprouted wheat
1 Small onion
½ cup diced celery
½ cup shredded carrots
1 cup almond butter
2 Ripe tomatoes

SAUCE
2 Ripe tomatoes
1 Cucumber
White Sesame Seeds
1 teaspoon garlic powder
½ cup water
1 teaspoon oregano
2 tablespoon Bronner's Bouillon

Cut Zucchini length-wise and hollow out. Blend stuffing ingredients and pat into each zucchini "boat". Blend sauce ingredients and pour over each zucchini. Serve as is or put in oven at 110° for ½-1 hour and serve.

SWEET POTATOE CROQUETTES

2 cups sweet potatoes, steamed and mashed
1 cup shredded carrots
1 cup minced celery
1 small onion, minced
2 cups cashew butter
minced parsley

Combine all ingredients except parsley. Pat into a 1-cup measuring cup to shape croquettes. Sprinkle parsley atop each croquette and serve.

SALADS

AMBROSIA

3 cups orange sections
4 cups pink and white grapefruit sections
3 bananas, peeled and sliced
1½ cups shredded coconut
1 box blueberries

Combine all ingredients except blueberries in serving dish. Refrigerate overnight. Garnish with blueberries just before serving.

ASSORTED SALAD

Lettuce
Cucumbers
Radishes
Green onions
Parsley
Celery

Wash clean two large heads of white lettuce, taking care to not break the leaves; peel and slice thinly two cucumbers of medium size. Put this in a bowl with teaspoonful of salt and a few lumps of ice for an hour before using. Peel and slice a few large-sized radishes. Decorate this with very small radishes. Leave in ice water until ready to use. Slice one small green onion, a little parsley chopped fine, and arrange these nicely upon a lettuce leaf and serve with dressing.

STUFFED PEPPERS

Cabbage
Celery
Onions
Salad Dressing
Green Peppers
Tomatoes
Lettuce

Take a little celery, cabbage, onions, a few green pepper seeds, a little fresh tomato, chopped fine, salt to taste. Stuff the peppers with this and serve on red cabbage leaves or lettuce, with Salad Dressing.

AVOCADO SUPREME

2 avocados, peeled and pitted
½ cup diced celery
garlic powder
½ cup almond butter
½ cup tofu mayonnaise
lettuce

Place two avocado halves on lettuce. Combine the remaining mashed avocado with other ingredients to make stuffing and serve.

AVOCADO AND TOMATO SPROUTED

2 chopped avocados
2 medium tomatoes, diced
1 small onion
¼ teaspoon oregano
¼ cup lemon juice
2 tablespoons Bronner's Bouillon
1 cup tofu mayonnaise

Toss and serve with:

½ cup sprouted sunflower seeds

BANANA SALAD

2 bananas, peeled and sliced
2 oranges, pared and diced
1 clump Thompson seedless grapes
1 cup pecans, coarsely grated
¼ cup shredded coconut

Mix all ingredients thoroughly and serve.

CABBAGE SALAD

1 head finely shredded cabbage, small

Mix the following in a bowl:
¼ teaspoon garlic powder
3 tablespoon lemon juice or according to taste
1 teaspoon salt
½ teaspoon onion powder

Pour over the cabbage, better the next day.

CARROT CABBAGE SALAD

2 cup chopped white cabbage
2 cup chopped red cabbage
1 cup diced celery
1 cup shredded carrot
½ cup raw sesame seed

Toss all ingredients and season with garlic, oregano, lemon juice and 1 cup Tofu mayonnaise and Dr. Bronner's seasoning.

CARROT SURPRISE

2 cups grated carrots
1 cup pineapple chunks
1 cup orange sections
1 cup diced apple
½ cup raisins
1 cup grated coconut
½ cup sunflower seeds
4 tablespoons tofu mayonnaise
Alfalfa sprouts

Combine all ingredients except sprouts. Refrigerate for one hour. Serve on bed of sprouts.

COLE SLAW

4 cups cabbage shredded
1 carrot, shredded
1 lemon, juiced
⅓ cup tofu mayonnaise
1 tablespoon honey
½ teaspoon celery seeds

Combine cabbage, carrot and lemon juice and let stand for 30 minutes. Blend mayonnaise, honey and celery seeds. Combine with cabbage mixture and blend well.

CUCUMBER, CELERY, AND CABBAGE SALAD

1 small cabbage
1 cucumber
3 green onions
1 green pepper
3 stalks celery
juice of one lemon or ¼ cup of tofu mayonnaise

Shred cabbage fine, mince onions, dice the cucumbers and cut the celery fine. Mix all ingredients and serve on bed of lettuce.

FINGER SALAD

6 Celery stalks
2 Tomatoes, sliced into wedges
1 Cucumber, cut into sticks
6 Carrots, cut into sticks
2 Avocados, peeled and sliced
8 radishes
1 Zucchini, cut into sticks
Lettuce
Parsley

Put lettuce on bottom of platter. Pile avocado in the center with tomato encircling avocado. Put remainder of ingredients in sections forming a circular design. Tofu mayonnaise and lemon wedges can be served with this salad as alternate dressings. A bed of alfalfa sprouts can be used as a substitute for the lettuce.

GRATED ROOT SALAD

1 cup grated turnip
1 cup grated parsnips
1 cup grated zucchini
½ cup grated red onion
1 cup diced tomatoes
1 cup Tofu mayonnaise

Toss all ingredients and serve in a lettuce-lined bowl. Garnish with raw sesame seeds sprinkled on top.

ITALIAN TOSSED SALAD

Lettuce (Romaine, Boston & Red Leaf)
Green onions (scallions)
Cucumbers, sliced
Parsley
Carrots, grated
Celery, cut into pieces
Radishes, sliced
Peppers

Toss together with lemon juice, garlic powder, oregano and very little salt. You may use Dr. Bronner's Bouillon and onion powder.

LENTIL SALAD

1½ cups dried lentils, sprouted
¾ cup water
1 small onion, chopped
1 bay leaf
2 cloves garlic
2 tablespoons Bronner's Bouillon
2 cups celery, chopped
½ cup green onions, chopped
2 tablespoons lemon juice
lettuce
sliced cucumber
tomato wedges

Combine all ingredients except lettuce, cucumber and tomato wedges. Cover and chill for several hours. Turn into bowl lined with salad greens, garnish with cucumber and tomatoes.

STUFFED AVOCADO

1⅓ cups lemon juice
1 tablespoon Bronner's Bouillon
1 tablespoon dill
¼ teaspoon onion powder
¼ teaspoon garlic powder
2 medium cucumbers, pared and thinly sliced
½ cup diced celery
1 diced tomato 3-4 unpeeled avocados, halved

Combine lemon juice and seasonings and pour over cucumbers and celery in shallow dish. Chill several hours or overnight, turning occasionally. Toss in tomato. Arrange half shells on salad greens and fill with mixture. May be garnished with watercress, parsley or alfalfa sprouts.

STUFFED CANTELOUPE

1 canteloupe, halved with seeds removed
2 strawberries, sliced
¼ cup sliced peaches
¼ cup blueberries
1 oz. unsweetened grated coconut
½-1 oz. chopped walnuts

Mix all ingredients well and stuff into each canteloupe half. You may top with honey if desired.

STUFFED PEARS

Large pears
Raisins
Apples
Chopped walnuts
Lettuce

Pare and core large pears. Mix equal amounts of raisins, apples, and walnuts. Serve on bed of lettuce.

TABBOULEH

1 cup wheat berries, soak in water 2 hours, finely chopped
½ cup red onion, finely chopped
2 tablespoons Bronner's Bouillon
1 tablespoon lemon juice
½ cup parsley, finely chopped
2 celery stalks, finely chopped
1½ cups tomatos, finely chopped
1 medium cucumber, diced
lettuce leaves

Soften wheat berries by soaking two hours in water. Drain well and press out excess moisture. Mix wheat berries, onions and Bronner's Bouillon, crushing berries and onions together with fork. Add lemon juice, parsley, tomatoes and cucumbers. Mix thoroughly. Serve on lettuce leaves.

TRUDIE'S FRUIT SALAD

In a large mixing bowl mix several varieties of fruit. Any unsweetened fruit, fresh or frozen, may be used, such as:

strawberries	blueberries
pitted dark sweet cherries	boysenberries
peaches	apricots
melons in season	sliced bananas

When using only fresh fruit add 1 small can fresh frozen unsweetened orange juice. Toss together.

Chop or fring in Moulinex ½ cup of each of the following, mix thoroughly together and keep refrigerated in a jar:

pecans	raw peanuts
sunflower seeds	walnuts
pumpkin seeds	powdered coconut

For an individual serving, arrange on plate in following order:

½ cup nut-seed mix
2 cups fruit mix
2 tsp. honey

It is delicious! Enjoy it! (This is a complete meal)

WALDORF SALAD

2 cups carrots
2 cups apples
1 cup raisins
1 cup chopped pineapple
1-2 cups Creamy Peanut Topping

Shred carrots and apples. Fold in raisins, pineapple, and Creamy Peanut Topping.

SOUPS

We do not interdict soups because they are not good food, but because they are swallowed without mastication. The objection to soup can be largely overcome by retaining it in the mouth long enough for it to become thoroughly or partially insalivated. This can be accomplished either by sipping it very slowly, or mixing with it very dry, hard foods — something that requires mastication.

It is a very foolish custom to make soup in a pot or kettle, when we remember that the only work that saliva and teeth were created to perform was that of making soup. Every particle of food taken into the mouth should be made into soup before it is swallowed. If this was done, indigestion, that great American disease, would disappear from the catalogue of human life.

We give here a few recipes for soups only because the soup habit is so firmly fixed in the mind of the housewife and the epicure that they can hardly conceive of a decent dinner without them. All soups may be warmed sufficiently to serve hot without cooking. Do not heat beyond 110°.

AVOCADO SOUP

4 ripened avocados
4 cups distilled or purified water
1 small onion
1 clove garlic
2 stalks celery
2 ripe tomatoes
¼ teaspoon oregano

Garnish with alfalfa sprouts. Liquify until smooth.

AVOCADO-TOMATO BLEND

4 medium tomatoes
½ cup grated carrots
½ cup grated celery
½ cup grated cabbage
1 whole avocado, diced
3 green onions, chopped
1 tablespoon Bronner's Bouillon
1 small bell pepper, chopped

Blend tomatoes and avocado first. Add other ingredients and blend to a thick consistency. For a variation add lemon juice.

CARROT SOUP

1 cup carrot juice
½ head cauliflower, chopped
1 cup celery
½ cup raw peanut meal
Watercress

Blend all ingredients except watercress to desired consistency. Garnish with watercress.

CASHEW CORN SOUP

4 cups cashew milk
1 package frozen corn or 2 cups fresh corn
1 green onion
1 avocado
1 teaspoon honey

Liquify in blender. May be served chilled or heated at low temperature.

COCONUT MILK SOUP

1 cup coconut milk
1 cup chopped fresh peaches
2 bananas
1 cup chopped apples with skins
1 cup chopped strawberries
Raisins for garnish

Blend all ingredients and pour into bowls. Garnish with raisins.

CREAM OF CORN SOUP

1 cup cashew milk
2 cups fresh cut corn
1 cup chopped celery
Parsley sprigs

Blend corn and cashew milk in blender until smooth. Add celery and garnish with parsley sprigs.

CREAM OF ONION SOUP

2 cups chopped onions
1 cup chopped carrots
1 cup diced celery
6 cups cashew or almond milk
¼ cup of avocado

Liquify all ingredients in blender. May be served chilled or heated at low temperature.

CREAMED ASPARAGUS SOUP

1 cup chopped asparagus
1 cup almond milk
1 cup fresh cut corn
1 cup chopped mushrooms
2 chopped scallions
1 tablespoon Bronner's Bouillon

Blend all ingredients to desired consistency and serve.

CREAMED VEGETABLE SOUP

4 medium tomatoes
1 cup almond milk
1 cup fresh cut corn
2 avocados, mashed
1 cup diced celery
1 cup grated carrots
3 scallions, diced

Blend tomatoes, milk, corn, and avocado. Add other ingredients and blend briefly to keep thick.

SPROUTED VEGETABLE SOUP

2 cups sprouted lentils
2 cups sprouted peas
1 cup fresh cut corn
2 celery stalks, diced
1 carrot, grated
1 clove garlic, minced
1 tablespoon Bronner's Bouillon
5 cups tomato juice

Blend all ingredients smooth except corn, which is to be stirred in at the end.

TOMATO SOUP

3 cups of unsweetened tomato juice
1 medium tomato
½ cucumber
1 medium carrot
1 small onion
¼ cup of cashew nut butter
¼ cup Italian seasoning

Put tomato juice in blender. Add chopped vegetables and nut butter. Liquify until finely chopped. Garnish with chopped alfalfa sprouts.

SPREADS

APPLE JAM

1 cup pulverized dried apples
1½ cups apple juice
½ teaspoon cinnamon
½ teaspoon allspice

Combine all ingredients in a bowl. Cover and refrigerate 24 hours and serve.

APPLE SAUCE

4 large apples, diced
½ cup unsweetened apple juice
½ cup raisins

Put juice in blender. Slowly add raisins at low speed followed by apples. Cloves and honey may be added for variety.

AVOCADO-SCALLION SPREAD

4 avocados, mashed
2 teaspoons Bronner's Bouillon
⅛ teaspoon oregano
2 tablespoons lemon juice
¼ cup chopped scallions (green onions)

Combine all ingredients. Cover and chill.

BANANA NUT CREAM SPREAD

2 cups raw peanut meal
4 large bananas, mashed
½ cup unsweetened apple juice

Put peanut meal and bananas in blender. Add enough apple juice to make a smooth spread. A sauce can be made by adding more apple juice.

CREAMY MUSHROOM SPREAD

4 cups mushrooms, scrubbed and chopped
1 cup Tofu Mayonnaise
2 scallions, chopped
1 avocado, mashed
1 teaspoon garlic powder
1 tablespoon Bronner's Bouillon

Mix or blend all ingredients until smooth.

DATE-NUT BUTTER

21 pitted dates
2 tablespoons almond meal
Unsweetened prune juice

Put dates in blender. Add enough prune juice to liquify and make a smooth, thick butter. Add almond meal and continue to blend until smooth.

NUT SPREAD

Grind 2 cups unroasted, unsalted nuts or seeds in nut grinder until fine. Put in container and mix with enough water to make a paste. May add 2-4 dates to sweeten if desired.

PEANUT BUTTER

#1 Blend 2 cups of steamed raw peanuts with two dates.

#2 Grind 2 cups raw peanuts to fine consistency. Add 1 teaspon raw honey with enough warm water to make a creamy paste.

SOY CHEESE

3 cups soybeans, sprouted until sprouts are length of beans
4 cups water
4 tablespoons lemon juice
1 teaspoon Bronner's Bouillon

Blend soybeans, Bouillon and water well. In cheesecloth, squeeze out the soy milk. Place in double boiler, stirring occasionally until 115°. Remove from stove and add lemon juice, lightly stirring. Strain through double cheesecloth-lined colander. When most of the whey has drained off, tie the corners of the cheesecloth together and hang an additional 90 minutes and cheese will be ready.

SPICY AVOCADO SPREAD

2 avocados, mashed
1 clove garlic, pressed
2 tablespoons Bronner's Bouillon
¼ cup Tofu mayonnaise
¼ cup diced red onion

Add all ingredients and stir with fork until well mixed.

SUNFLOWER SEED BLEND

2 cups sunflower sprouts
1 cored apple
½ canteloupe, cubed
2 tablespoons apple juice
1 cup crushed pineapple

Blend all ingredients until smooth. Refrigerate and serve.

TOMATO-BARLEY SPREAD

1 cup ripe tomatoes
½ cup water
¼ cup lemon juice
1 teaspoon garlic powder
1 teaspoon onion powder
1 teaspoon oregano or chives
1 cup barley flour

Blend all ingredients until smooth.

BREADS

CORNBREAD

2 cups bolted cornmeal
1 cup rolled oat flour
¼ cup each: finely ground cashew nuts, sunflower seeds, sesame seeds
3 tablespoons honey
¼ cup almond butter

Mix dry ingredients. Add honey. Knead in nut butter. Add just enough water to make a dough. Form into loaf. Wrap in wax paper and store in refrigerator. Slice to serve.

CORN CHIPS

2 cups fresh cut corn
½ teaspoon onion powder
½ teaspoon garlic powder
½ teaspoon Bronner's Bouillon
3 tablespoons chopped fresh tomatoes
3 tablespoons chives

Blend all ingredients except tomato and chives. Pour onto leather drying sheets or plastic wrap. Top with tomato and chives. Dry until crisp and break into chips.

DATE-NUT SPREAD

2 cups rolled oats
3 dates
1 cup apple juice
¼ cup almond meal
¼ cup walnut meal

Put dates with apple juice and blend. Add oats and soak 1 hour. Add remaining ingredients. Form into roll. Put in sun, food dryer, or oven at 110°, 2 hours.

FRUIT BREAD

1 cup chopped dates
1 cup chopped apricots
1 cup finely chopped walnuts
2 mashed bananas
2 cups raw peanut flour (or meal)
2 cups oat flour
Water if necessary

Combine all ingredients and knead well. Shape into wafers and bake ½ to 1 hour in oven at 110°, turning once.

GARLIC CRACKERS

3 garlic cloves, minced
3 cups soaked wheatberries
½ cup minced celery
½ cup minced onion

Mix and put all ingredients through a food grinder. Roll out flat between 2 sheets of wax paper. Remove the top sheet and place in (1) Sun, (2) food dryer at 100° until firm, or (3) oven at 105° until crisp.

NUT OATMEAL BREAD

¼ cup finely ground pecans
¼ cup finely ground almonds
¼ cup finely ground unsalted raw peanuts
1 cup oatmeal
½ cup raw peanut butter
4 dates

Mix ingredients and put through food grinder for a second time. Add water and form into loaf. Wrap in wax paper and store in refrigerator. Slice when ready to serve.

SPROUTED WALNUT-OAT BREAD

2 cups sprouted oats
½ cup chopped walnuts
1 tablespoon rye seed
1 teaspoon Bronner's Bouillon
Oat flour, if necessary, for binding

Fine grind oats. Mix all ingredients and knead. Form into loaf and bake in oven 2 hours at 110°.

SPROUTED WHEAT CRACKERS

2 cups sprouted wheat berries
1 teaspoon Bronner's Bouillon
½ cup applesauce
Berry soaking water

Soak and sprout wheat 24 hours. Grind berries fine, work into a dough with Bouillon. Add applesauce and soak water to make a thick cream.

Dryer: Cover a non-stick cookie sheet with dryer sheet and spread dough over it. Dehydrate at 100° oven.

Oven: Spread out on non-stick cookie sheet and bake until dry in 110° oven.

DESSERTS

APPLE PIE

Filling:
4 cups grated apples
¼ cup honey
½ teaspoon cinnamon
½ teaspoon nutmeg
½ cup cashew butter

Mix all ingredients and put in pie crust.

Basic Pie Crust:
½ cup ground sunflower seed
½ cup ground raw peanuts
½ cup ground unsweetened coconut
¼ cup almond butter
2 tablespoons honey
¼ cup oat flour
1 cup oatmeal
4 tablespoons purified water

Mix dry ingredients. Knead in almond butter and honey. Put the mixture through the food grinder. Add water to make dough. Roll out on waxed paper. Place in pie plate. Bake at 105° until crust is firm.

BANANA CREAM PIE FILLING

2 bananas, peeled
4 bananas, peeled and sliced
½ cup apple juice
½ cup shredded coconut
1 tablespoon honey
2 dates

Blend the two peeled bananas and other ingredients in blender, reserving the sliced bananas. Gently mix in an additional ½ cup coconut and banana slices. Chill to set before serving.

BLUEBERRY ICE CREAM

Use: Food Processor, bottom blade

2 frozen bananas
1 pint frozen blueberries
⅞ cup cashew milk
1 teaspoon vanilla
1 teaspoon almond flavoring

1. Blueberries on bottom
2. Add bananas
3. Add remaining ingredients.

Serve and enjoy!

BLUEBERRY PIE

3 cups fresh or frozen blueberries
½ cup pecan meal
¼ cup pitted dates
¼ cup almond butter
½ cup prune juice
½ teaspoon soy flour
½ teaspoon nutmeg

Soften dates in warm water by placing dates in jar which is set in bowl of warm water. Mash with fork. Add soy flour. Gradually add water until mixture is of right consistency to make a medium thick filling. Add pecan meal and mix until smooth. Fold in blueberries. Fill pie crust and put in freezer for two hours. Serve chilled.

CAROB BUTTER BALLS

1 cup raw peanut butter
½ cup raisins
½ cup unsweetened coconut, grated
4 tablespoons raw unsweetened carob powder
1 tablespoon raw honey

Stir all ingredients together and form into balls. Refrigerate and serve.

COVERED FROZEN BANANAS

Carob Powder
Raw peanut or raw cashew butter
Ripe bananas
Chopped nuts

1. Peel and slice bananas in half down the middle. Place on cookie sheet and freeze.

2. Mix carob powder with peanut butter to taste.

3. Remove frozen bananas from freezer and cover with nut butter mixture.

4. Roll covered bananas in nuts and refreeze until mealtime.

CREAMY PEACH PIE

4 cups fresh peaches
3 teaspoons Agar-Agar
½ cup Milky Way Beverage
1 medium peach, pitted
2 tablespoons honey
1 teaspoon allspice

Dissolve Agar-Agar according to package directions. Add to Beverage in blender. Blend together, adding other ingredients. Fill in pie crust and chill until firm.

FROZEN FRUIT BARS

JUICES:

1. Unsweetened apple juice
2. Unsweetened cranberry juice
3. Unsweetened pineapple juice

FRUITS:
1. Chopped strawberries, blueberries, peaches, apricots
2. Chopped bananas
3. Chopped mango, pineapple, bananas

In a frozen bar maker or ice-tray, select a fruit and fill it half-way up, following the remaining half with its corresponding juice. If put in an ice-tray, use large plastic cocktail toothpicks in each section of the tray and place in the center. Freeze until stiff and serve.

FRUIT TART

Shredded coconut
banana slices
strawberries, sliced
blueberries, whole
peaches, peeled and sliced
kiwi fruit, peeled and sliced

3 teaspoons Agar-Agar
½ cup apple juice

Line quiche dish with basic crust. Start design by arranging banana slices forming an "X" in dish. Add a row of fruit to the right of each banana border leaving the blueberries for last.

Dissolve Agar-Agar according to package directions. Put in blender with apple juice. Pour over tart. Freeze for two hours and serve chilled.

MARK'S BANANA SPLIT

1 banana, peeled and sliced in half
raw peanut, cashew or sesame butter
bee pollen
raw honey
Iron Recipe topping
shredded coconut

Start by spreading the nut butter on each banana half. Follow on one half of banana with the bee pollen and honey; top with other banana half. Cover the banana with Iron Recipe or strawberry topping. Garnish with coconut and serve.

NO-BAKE CARROT CAKE

1. 1 cup rolled oats
   ½ cup miller's bran
   ½ cup sunflower seed meal
   1 teaspoon cinnamon
   ½ teaspoon nutmeg
   ½ teaspoon allspice
   ½ cup unsweetened shredded coconut

2. ¼ cup honey
   1 teaspoon vanilla
   3 tablespoons water
   3 tablespoons raw applesauce
   ½ cup almond butter

3. ½ cup raisins
   ½ cup dates
   3 cups carrots

Mix #1 ingredients in a bowl and keep separate. In another bowl mix #2 ingredients. Put #3 ingredients through the food grinder. Mix the ground carrot mixture with honey mixture and put through the food grinder a second time. Form into loaf. Refrigerate two hours, unmold and garnish with coconut and ground nuts.

PEACH ICE CREAM

5 large peaches, chopped
5 bananas, peeled
½ cup almond milk
1 tablespoon honey

Blend all ingredients until smooth. Freeze until set (4-5 hours) and serve.

PEANUT BUTTER COOKIES

1 cup raw peanut butter
1 cup raisins
1 cup dates
1 cup ground raw peanuts
1 teaspoon vanilla
½ cup soy flour
1 cup oatmeal
Shredded coconut

Put raisins and dates through food grinder and mix with other ingredients except coconut. Roll out on waxed paper. Then roll on coconut. Refrigerate until ready to serve. Serve in slices.

RAISIN COCONUT COOKIES

2 cups ground raisins
2 cups finely ground coconut
4 cups 24-hour sprouted wheat, ground
1 cup chopped pecans
¼ teaspoon each: cinnamon, nutmeg, allspice
1 teaspoon honey

Mix all ingredients together and knead well to make a stiff dough. Pat to ½ inch thick on a non-stick cookie sheet and cut into 2-inch squares.

1. Refrigerate until ready to serve.

2. Put in oven at 110° until set, ½-1 hour.

SOY CHEESECAKE

2 tablespoons Agar
½ cup hot (not boiling) water
½ cup almond milk
3 tablespoons honey
2 teaspoons lemon juice
¾ teaspoon pure vanilla
1½ cups sprouted soy cheese (one recipe)
½ cup unsweetened coconut meal
¼ cup miller's bran
¼ cup mashed banana

Dissolve Agar in water and add the almond milk, warmed over a double boiler. Stir well and cool until it begins to thicken. Blend all ingredients except coconut and bran. Add Agar mixture and blend one-half minute. Separately combine coconut and bran. Sprinkle half over bottom of pie plate. Turn Agar mixture into pan and sprinkle remaining coconut mixture on top. Freeze or chill until firm and serve.

TOPPINGS

CREAMY LEMON AND HONEY SPREAD

1 cup lemon juice
3 tablespoons honey
2 cups almond or raw peanut butter or
　1 cup soaked oats
Purified water, if necessary

Blend all ingredients to desired consistency. More lemon juice and water may be added to make a sauce for fruit dishes.

PINEAPPLE TOPPING

2 cups unsweetened crushed pineapple
1 teaspoon vanilla
raw peanut meal

Put pineapple and vanilla in blender. Add peanut meal until of thick consistency. Refrigerate until ready to serve.

STRAWBERRY TOPPING

1 box strawberries
water
honey to taste

Wash and clean strawberries. Put in bowl with enough water to cover half the strawberries and soak for 1-2 hours. Mash strawberries and add honey to taste.

TARTER SAUCE

1 cup Tofu Mayonnaise
3 tablespoons lemon juice
½ cup diced cucumber
½ small onion, diced
⅛ cup finely chopped parsley

Mix together. May be served on loafs or patties.

HONEY-HERB SALAD DRESSING

½ cup lemon juice
½ cup honey
Hidden Valley Ranch Dressing to taste

Keep in shaker-top bottle in refrigerator. This is a delicious sweet and sour dressing.

TOFU MAYONNAISE

Blend:

1 whole block of tofu
⅓-½ cup lemon juice
½ teaspoon oregano
½ teaspoon sweet basil
½ teaspoon garlic powder
½ teaspoon onion powder

TOFU SALAD DRESSING

¼ cup raw sunflower seed meal (or cashew nuts)
Juice of four (4) medium-sized lemons
2 cups tofu
2-3 tablespoons Bronner's Bouillon
¼ teaspoon garlic powder
water

Blend ingredients until well mixed. Start with ¼ cup water and add to desired consistency.

TWO TOPPINGS IN ONE!

1. **IRON BUILDER:**
   Soak Dr. Hoffman's Iron Recipe as follows:
   1-2 cups prunes
   1 cup unsulphured apricots
   1 cup Black Mission figs
   1 cup seedless Monukka raisins

Rinse above fruit in colander or large sieve under a strong spray. Remove the stems from the Black Mission figs, put the fruit into a half-gallon jar, fill the balance of the jar with unsweetened apple juice. Let stand at room temperature for 24 hours.

Drain 2 cups of liquid from fruit for topping as follows and use fruit to top breakfast cereal or dessert!

2. **CREAMY PEANUT TOPPING**
   2 cups Iron Recipe juice
   1 tablespoon honey
   1 cup raw peanut butter

Liquify until well blended and serve with melon, fruit salad, or puddings.

BEVERAGES

ALMOND MILK

1 cup raw almonds
1 quart water
¼ teaspoon salt or ¼ teaspoon Bronner's Bouillon
1 teaspoon vanilla (optional)
3 dates, pitted and chopped

Put nuts, salt, dates, and 1½-2 cups water in blender and blend until smooth. Pour into container and add remaining water. Shake well before pouring into serving glass as it will settle.

BANANA CANTELOUPE FREEZE

2 cups Milky Way Recipe
2 ripe bananas, peeled
½ medium sliced canteloupe, peeled and sliced
2-3 ice cubes
1 teaspoon honey

Blend slowly in electric blender for ten seconds, and then blend for 30 more seconds at the highest speed.

BANANA DELIGHT

Blend together:

1 ripe banana
1 cup strawberries (fresh or frozen, unsweetened)
1 cup peaches
3 cups apple juice (unsweetened)

BARLEY-DATE DRINK

2 glasses apple juice
1-2 bananas
2-2½ tablespoons barley
3-5 dates

Soak apple juice, barley and dates overnight. Put in blender with bananas and blend until smooth.

Substitutions: Water for apple juice
                 Black Mission Figs for dates

CAROB MALT

4 tablespoons carob powder
2 cups almond milk
½ cup shredded coconut
2 bananas, peeled and sliced
3 dates, soaked and diced

Blend all ingredients until smooth. Start with milk and carob powder. Then add other ingredients.

CASHEW MILK

1 cup raw cashews
1 quart water
¼ teaspoon salt or ¼ teaspoon Bronner's Bouillon
1 teaspoon vanilla (optional)
3 dates, pitted and chopped

Put nuts, salt, dates, and 1½ to 2 cups water in blender and blend until smooth. Pour into container and add remaining water. Shake well before pouring into serving glass as it will settle.

CRANBERRY PUNCH

1 cup raw almonds
½ cup hazelnuts
1 cup raisins
1 apple, chopped
1 teaspoon whole cloves
½ teaspoon whole allspices
1 stick cinnamon
1 quart water (warm)
2 quarts cranberry juice
1 quart unsweetened pineapple juice
2 cups orange juice

Put nuts and raisins in bowl with chopped apple. Tie spices in cheesecloth and place in bowl. Cover ingredients with warm water and soak for two hours. Discard the spice bag and combine liquid and fruit with juices.

FASTER'S DREAM

½ glass carrot juice
½ glass celery juice

GARDEN COCKTAIL

Blend together:

4 cups sugar-free tomato juice
1 medium cucumber
1 medium red onion
1 clove garlic
¼ cup parsley
2 ripe tomatoes

MANGO SMOOTHIE

1 mango
1 banana
1 cup apple juice
½ cup coconut meal

Blend all ingredients until smooth.

MILK

Try the Cashew Milk recipe, adding 1 cup dried or fresh bananas.

THE MILKY WAY

½ cup cashew butter
1 cup soaked oatmeal with 3 dates (soaked)
1 teaspoon vanilla
4 cups warm water

Combine all ingredients in blender and serve.

ORANGE FREEZE

3 cups fresh squeezed orange juice
1 cup fresh peeled and slices peaches
2 bananas, peeled
6 ice cubes

Place all ingredients in a blender and whip until well mixed and frothy.

TROPICAL DREAM

Blend together:

1 cup fresh pineapple (or small can, unsweetened crushed pineapple)
1 banana
2 cups pineapple juice or apple juice or apricot nectar (unsweetened)
Water from inside of coconut (save coconut for Tropical Salad)

VEGETABLE INSTRUCTIONS

Vegetables occupy a very important place in the elementary food menu. They contain elements that cannot be secured elsewhere.

When thoroughly masticated, in addition to their nutritive value, they serve the body as an alimentary lubricant. No meal can be made complete without some green plant.

CELERY

Wash, trim and scrape the stalks, selecting those that are green and tender. Should be placed in refrigerator crisper until they are wanted, which makes them very crisp.

COLE SLAW

There is nothing more delicious or necessary than shredded cabbage, usually called cole slaw. It possesses valuable food properties, occupying the same place in human diet that hay does in diet of the horse or cow.

LETTUCE

Lettuce is undoubtedly the best of salads. Wash each leaf separately. Place lettuce in single layers on paper towels to dry. Stack several layers one on top of the other. Place in Tupperware or any similar container and keep refrigerated until ready to use. With the lid tightly covered it will stay fresh for many days. When making a tossed salad, lettuce should be the last thing cut.

CARROTS AND TURNIPS

Are very nice cut into cubes and served on a lettuce leaf with or without a salad dressing.

FRESH TOMATOES

Cut with a very sharp knife. Slice and cover with Honey-Herb Salad Dressing or with plain yogurt containing acidophilus culture into which has been added Hidden Valley Ranch Dressing to taste.

SWEET CORN

This thoroughly masticated will be found a most delicious and nourishing dish. Sweet corn is a very good source of fiber which is very important to our health.

FRESH GREEN PEAS

Take quantity desired, hull, rinse. Fresh green peas are most delicious, high in nutrients and chlorophyll.

CUCUMBERS

Take number desired. Slice thin. Soak in Hidden Valley Ranch Dressing 1-2 hours before serving.

OLIVES

Olives are a very important article in the elementary menu. The cured olive, extensively used, is in reality much superior to the green. If you would like to cure your own olives, the instructions for this are found in my Grandmother's cookbook entitled NO OIL, NO FAT VEGETARIAN COOKBOOK.

RADISHES — CARROTS — ONIONS — YAMS
TURNIPS — BEETS — GREEN PEPPERS

These articles can be ground in a vegetable mill altogether, or they can be eaten separately. If ground together by the addition of nuts they compose a very nourishing and necessary article of diet.

NUTS AND CARROTS

Put two medium carrots and a half cup of pecan meats through a fine vegetable grinder; moisten with yogurt containing acidophilus culture, set on a stove a few minutes (must not exceed 110º). Serve.

SUN-COOKED CORN

Cut sweet corn from the cob with a dull knife, scraping out the germ of the corn, creating a milky substance. Dry this thoroughly in the sun. Put in small cloth bags for future use. To prepare for table, place quantity to be used in a deep vessel, almost cover with warm water. Put in a cool place and let stand overnight. Then add a small quantity of yogurt with acidophilus culture about 2 hours before serving warm (not over 110º).